W9-AAK-852

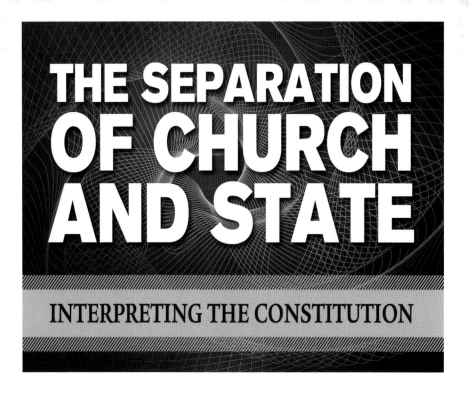

THE SEPARATION OF CHURCH AND STATE

INTERPRETING THE CONSTITUTION

JASON PORTERFIELD

ROSEN
PUBLISHING®

New York

Published in 2015 by The Rosen Publishing Group, Inc.
29 East 21st Street, New York, NY 10010

First Edition

Library of Congress Cataloging-in-Publication Data

Porterfield, Jason.
The separation of church and state : interpreting the Constitution/Jason Porterfield.
    pages cm. — (Understanding the United States
    Constitution)
Includes bibliographical references and index.
ISBN 978-1-4777-7508-0 (library bound)
1. Church and state—United States—History—Juvenile literature. 2. Religion and politics—United States—History—Juvenile literature. 3. Freedom of religion—United States—History—Juvenile literature. 4. Religion in the public schools—United States—History—Juvenile literature. I. Title.
BR516.P675 2015
342.7308'52—dc23
                           2013044754

Manufactured in China

CONTENTS

The first ten amendments to the United States Constitution are referred to collectively as the Bill of Rights. They protect basic liberties, including religious freedom.

I

n May 2013, the U.S. Supreme Court announced that it would hear the case *Galloway v. Town of Greece* during its nine-month term beginning that October. It would be the latest in the Court's long history to deal with the separation of church and state.

The case revolved around the Greece, New York, town board's use of prayer at the opening of each meeting. Volunteers from the town read the prayers. In 2008, two residents sued the town, claiming the practice violated the First Amendment by endorsing religion. They further argued that the majority of prayers recited were Christian prayers. When they complained, they were told they could leave the room during the prayers. The town responded to the suit by inviting people from a broader range of faiths to read prayers, but it stood by the practice.

The Second U.S. Circuit Court of Appeals ruled that the prayer policy violated the Constitution by endorsing Christianity because the process of picking someone to lead the prayers essentially ensured that a Christian viewpoint would be expressed. When the Supreme Court hears the case, the justices will have to decide if the prayers really were an endorsement of Christianity. They might ask whether the town did enough to make sure that other faiths were represented and whether people in the audience were coerced to take part.

The separation of church and state has its origins in the Bill of Rights, which prohibits the federal government from establishing a national religion, or favoring certain established religions, through the establishment clause of the First Amendment. Later, the prohibition against establishing religions was extended to state and local governments. Beginning in the twentieth century, a number of Supreme Court cases set guidelines for keeping church and state separate. Schools, public holiday displays, and town meetings such as those in the town of Greece have been affected by rulings in which religious expression in the public realm has been ruled constitutional or unconstitutional.

CHAPTER ONE

A NEW NATION OF FAITHS

Many early colonists came to North America during times of religious conflict in Europe. Some had been persecuted for their beliefs in their home countries, while others simply wanted the freedom to openly practice their religion. They brought a wide range of faiths with them. Protestant denominations were the most widespread. In some colonies, tax money helped fund churches and religious activities. While some colonies practiced religious tolerance, others passed laws that discriminated against those of the Jewish and Catholic faiths, while Native Americans and black slaves were often forced to convert to Christianity.

Colonial leaders, including Thomas Jefferson and James Madison, were inspired to push for religious freedom. Jefferson wrote the Virginia

This statue of President Thomas Jefferson is located in his Washington, D.C., memorial. Jefferson believed that people should have the right to worship as they wished, without government interference.

Statute for Religious Freedom shortly after drafting the Declaration of Independence in 1776. With this document, Jefferson sought to guarantee religious freedom for people of all faiths and separate the Church of England from Virginia's government. Jefferson held complex religious beliefs and was passionate about keeping religion and government separate. He did not want a government that would encourage or force its people to belong to one particular religion or favor one faith above all others. Jefferson's opponents attacked the document, with some of his enemies accusing him of not believing in God. The Virginia General Assembly tabled the bill.

In 1785, Governor Patrick Henry was trying to pass a bill that would have taxed citizens in order to pay teachers at religious schools. James Madison wrote an essay, titled "Memorial and Remonstrance Against Religious Assessments," arguing against the bill and for the separation of church and state. Madison put forth several arguments for keeping religion separate from government, gathering the signatures of two thousand people. The lawmakers saw that public opinion was against the bill and set it aside. Instead, they voted to pass Jefferson's Statute for Religious Freedom, which became law in 1786, making Virginia the first state to formally separate church and state.

DRAFTING THE CONSTITUTION

The 1780s were a difficult time for the fledgling United States of America. The new nation had just endured a lengthy fight for independence from Great Britain. Its previous form of government, organized around a document called the Articles of Confederation, had failed to bring the thirteen colonies together. Many of the leaders of the American Revolution feared their cause was doomed if they couldn't unite.

Leaders from each state, many of whom had been active in the revolutionary cause, met in Philadelphia, Pennsylvania, in 1787 to work out a form of government that would keep the new nation together without violating the rights of individual states. Months of negotiations led to the drafting of the U.S. Constitution, which outlined the democratic government that would govern the nation.

The Constitution itself, however, is almost silent on the issue of whether religion and government should be separated. The document's Framers didn't want to establish any laws that might infringe upon the rights of the states. The one instance in which religion is referenced occurs in Article VI, which establishes the Constitution as the "supreme Law of the Land." One clause of the article contains language forbidding the use of a person's religion as a disqualifier from holding elected office or a government position.

Members of the U.S. House of Representatives are sworn in before their first session in 2011. The U.S. Constitution guarantees that members of any religion can hold elected office.

THE BILL OF RIGHTS

Even as the Constitution was ratified by individual states and became the law of the land in 1788, some leaders thought the document needed to be more specific about the rights protected by it. In response, Madison, with input from others, drew up the Bill of Rights, which was designed to protect certain freedoms from interference on the part of the federal government.

Prominent among those rights was the freedom for individuals to practice religion as they saw fit. Many colonists had originally come to North America from Europe to escape religious persecution. They didn't want to see an official state religion established that might discriminate against members of their own faith. Religious freedom is mentioned in the First Amendment, which also guarantees protection for the freedoms of speech and assembly. Madison used the Virginia Statute for Religious Freedom as a guide when writing the amendment.

At the time it was ratified in 1791, the Bill of Rights was one of the earliest documents to guarantee religious freedom. Although the establishment clause of the First Amendment states that "Congress shall make no law respecting an establishment of religion, or

Like his mentor Thomas Jefferson, James Madison felt that religion and government should be kept separate.

prohibiting the free exercise thereof," it does not say outright that religion and government must be separated. This has led to a lot of uncertainty over how the clause should be interpreted.

The language in the Bill of Rights was intentionally vague. The Framers of the Constitution had envisioned a nation with a weak central government and strong state governments. They wanted to leave enough room for individual states to make their own interpretations while offering protection to the freedoms of citizens.

The U.S. Supreme Court has ruled that the establishment clause does not allow the federal government to interfere with a person's exercise of religious beliefs. Neither does it permit any one religion to be given a show of preference over others.

EARLY INTERPRETATIONS

During the early days of the nation, U.S. presidents Thomas Jefferson and James Madison produced documents that have been used as guideposts for future decisions on the separation of church and state. Madison wrote widely on the issue throughout his later life, but it was Jefferson who made the greater impact with a letter he wrote in 1802.

THE TREATY OF TRIPOLI

As the nation's second president, John Adams followed George Washington's example by holding public prayer days and feasts of thanksgiving. However, Adams was not a strong believer in religion having a role in government. His official stance was called into question when he signed the 1797 Treaty of Tripoli.

Adams signed the treaty as a way to protect U.S. ships from pirates operating out of the nation-state of Tripoli, now part of modern-day Libya. The treaty with the Muslim nation stated that the government of the United States was "not, in any sense, founded on the Christian religion" and declared that "no pretext arising from religious opinions shall ever produce an interruption of the harmony existing between the two countries."

The language in the treaty has been used by some to argue that the nation's founders intended a strict separation of church and state. Still others have dismissed it as an insignificant work of diplomacy.

The letter was a response to a group called the Danbury Baptist Association of Danbury, Connecticut. The Baptists, who were a religious minority in Connecticut at the time, had written to Jefferson shortly after he became president in 1801 to complain that their state legislature did not treat their religious freedom as a right but as a privilege. In his response to them, Jefferson said it would violate the establishment clause for him or Congress to intervene on their behalf and that the clause built what he called "a wall of separation between church and state."

A copy of Jefferson's response was later published in

Above is an original draft of Jefferson's letter to the Danbury Baptists. The letter would later have a major impact on many court rulings concerning the separation of church and state.

a Boston newspaper, making the president's thoughts on the separation of church and state widely known. The letter would later become a pivotal point in court rulings on church and state, and it would go on to influence future presidents—particularly Jefferson's successor, James Madison. During his presidency, Madison vetoed two bills that he believed would have violated the establishment clause.

CHAPTER TWO

RELIGION IN THE NINETEENTH CENTURY

In the late eighteenth and early nineteenth centuries, religion played an important part in the lives of Americans. From approximately 1790 to 1840, the United States experienced the Second Great Awakening, when church membership increased significantly among Protestant denominations. Immigrants adhering to non-Protestant faiths who continued to arrive on America's shores often faced religious intolerance, particularly Catholics and Jews. The traditional beliefs of Native Americans and black slaves were marginalized or suppressed, and efforts were made to convert members of these groups to Christianity. Protestant denominations continued to grow throughout the century, while immigrants from Europe and Asia brought their religious beliefs with them. By the end of the nineteenth century, Catholicism would become the country's largest Christian denomination.

There was little public debate over church and state issues for the first half of the nineteenth century. Yet events were taking place that would influence the course of the debate for years to come.

AN ERA OF SOCIAL MOVEMENTS

Several social movements were under way in the United States at this time. Many of these movements took advantage of the social structure of churches in communities across the country to attract more followers.

The temperance movement, which worked to ban the sale, manufacture, and distribution of alcohol, was led by evangelical Christians who

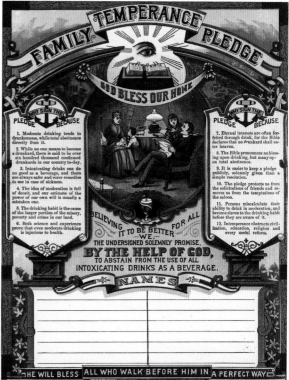

Seen here is a temperance pledge from the early 1900s. The temperance movement to ban the sale of alcohol was largely driven by churches and religious groups.

believed that many of society's ills were caused by alcohol. Movement advocates often turned to scripture to make their point. In 1919, the Eighteenth Amendment to the Constitution made it illegal to produce or sell alcohol. The amendment was repealed by the Twenty-First Amendment in 1933.

At the time, women were not allowed to cast ballots in most elections. The suffrage movement, which began in 1848 in Seneca Falls, New York, drew some of the same members as efforts to abolish slavery and the sale of alcohol. The suffragists succeeded in winning the right for women to vote with the ratification of the Nineteenth Amendment in 1919.

Abolitionists stressed that slavery was morally wrong. Seeking to end slavery in the United States, proponents of the abolitionist movement used passages from the Bible in an attempt to convince church congregations to follow their movement.

EXPANDING THE ESTABLISHMENT CLAUSE

Of the social movements tied to religion, the effort to abolish slavery had the greatest impact on the separation of church and state. During the American Civil War, in 1863, President Abraham Lincoln issued the Emancipation Proclamation, which freed people held as slaves in the rebelling Southern states, provided that

The Emancipation Proclamation began a move toward the abolition of slavery. Ending slavery eventually led to expansion of the establishment clause to include coverage of state laws.

STATES AND THE BILL OF RIGHTS

Prior to the ratification of the Fourteenth Amendment and the development of the incorporation doctrine, the Supreme Court in 1833 held in *Barron v. Baltimore* that the Bill of Rights applied only to the federal government, not state governments. The case involved a merchant named John Barron, who owned a wharf in Baltimore's harbor. Barron sued the mayor of Baltimore because deposits of sand and earth from a city construction project had made the harbor near his wharf too shallow for ships to enter and dock. He argued that the action violated the Fifth Amendment to the Bill of Rights because the city had essentially taken his property in order to complete its project without compensating him.

The Court ruled unanimously that the Fifth Amendment applied only to the federal government and the freedoms guaranteed by the Bill of Rights did not restrict state governments. This interpretation would remain dominant until the twentieth century.

Union forces won the war. Slavery was formally abolished in the United States after the war had ended, with the ratification of the Thirteenth Amendment in 1865.

The Fourteenth Amendment followed in 1868, expanding citizenship rights and equal protection under the law to all citizens, specifically freed slaves. The amendment forbade individual states from enacting laws that infringed on their constitutional rights. One key outcome of the amendment was the extension of the establishment clause to the states. Previously, the constitutional prohibition against establishing a formal religion had only applied to federal laws, leaving state laws exempt.

THE FIRST BIG TEST

The U.S. Supreme Court heard its first case dealing with the separation of church and state in 1878, just a few years after the Fourteenth Amendment was ratified. The case of *Reynolds v. United States* touched on both the freedom to worship and the rights of the government to pass laws restricting some religious practices.

The case centered upon the recently formed Church of Jesus Christ of Latter-day Saints (the Mormon Church), which was founded in 1830 by Joseph Smith in upstate New York. The church's separate religious texts and teachings set it apart from established Christian denominations; its followers often faced persecution. Even as its membership grew, the church was forced to relocate several times, in several states, to avoid persecution before finally finding a home in present-day Utah.

One of the church's most controversial practices was bigamy, in which a man was allowed to be married to more than one woman at a time. The practice

This portrait is of a nineteenth-century Mormon family. The former church practice of bigamy was at the heart of the first Supreme Court case concerning the separation of church and state.

was banned by federal law, and in 1874, a man named George Reynolds was arrested and charged with bigamy after he married a second wife. Reynolds and the church challenged the law, arguing that he was following the teachings of his church and that the law infringed upon his constitutional right to religious freedom.

The justices disagreed and ruled against him. Relying on the writings of Jefferson and Madison for guidance, they determined that while the Constitution does guarantee free practice of religion, it does not necessarily allow defendants in criminal cases to use their faith as a defense. While the ruling was important and would have an impact on later cases, the deliberations of the justices proved just as vital to future interpretations of the establishment clause.

CHAPTER THREE

TESTING LEGAL WATERS

A number of cases concerning the separation of church and state came before the Supreme Court in the twentieth century. Some involved citizens protesting their right to practice their religion. Others contested the use of public money to support secular causes. Then there were cases whose arguments were fomented in classrooms across the United States.

RELIGION, NOT SOLICITATION

In the late 1930s, a Jehovah's Witness named Newton Cantwell and his two sons were going door to door in New Haven, Connecticut, with pamphlets and books. They were attempting to spread the word about their faith, but they also angered many residents in the Roman Catholic neighborhood where they were conducting their recruiting efforts. They were eventually arrested and charged with causing a breach of the peace

Jehovah's Witnesses share their message of faith in the 1950s. The Supreme Court ruled in 1940 that such visits are protected by the First Amendment.

and violating a state law that required people who solicited door to door to get a special certificate from the state's public welfare council before they could ask for money.

The Cantwells argued in court that they did not get a certificate because they did not feel it was the government's place to say whether the Jehovah's Witnesses qualified as a religion. Besides, they hadn't been asking for money. They based their defense on the argument that the state law violated their right to due process under the Fourteenth Amendment and their First Amendment right to freedom of speech and religious expression. The Connecticut Supreme Court sided against them, stating that the law was constitutional because it was intended to protect the public from fraud.

The Cantwells took the case to the U.S. Supreme Court in 1940, where the justices ruled unanimously that their actions were indeed protected by the Constitution and that the state law violated their rights. The case was the Court's first significant ruling on the separation of church and state and freedom of religion.

The Supreme Court's ruling strengthened religious freedom by stating that religious activities were protected against state and local laws, as well as against federal statutes. It would be far from the last case on the matter, however. The following decades would see a number of Supreme Court cases that would define the limits of state control over religion and the part that faith could play in the public sphere.

INCORPORATING
THE CONSTITUTION

The act of making elements of the Constitution apply broadly to state and local laws is called incorporation. *Cantwell v. Connecticut* was significant because it incorporated the First Amendment's free exercise clause, something the Court ruling in *Reynolds v. United States* did not accomplish.

Even though the Fourteenth Amendment applied the Bill of Rights to state and local laws, for decades the Supreme Court held that the First and Second amendments did not apply to state governments. This began changing during the 1920s, when the Court started interpreting the Fourteenth Amendment more broadly and incorporating more portions of the Bill of Rights.

NEXT ON THE DOCKET

The 1947 Supreme Court case *Everson v. Board of Education* was the next landmark ruling to deal with the separation of church and state. The case came about when a New Jersey taxpayer named Arch R. Everson sued his local school district to block it from using tax money to repay money spent by parents who had to use public transportation to send their children to private religious schools. At that time, states were allowed to grant privileges to religious denominations.

Everson felt that by using taxpayer money in this way, the school district was violating the First Amendment and the due process clause of the Fourteenth Amendment, which requires states to respect all legal rights guaranteed to citizens under the Bill of Rights.

The result of the case was mixed, as the justices split on whether the payments to parents violated the Constitution. They ultimately ruled 5–4 that they were constitutional because the payments were not related to the religious function of the school. However, all nine justices agreed that the Constitution called for a distinct separation of church and state. In their opinion, they cited Jefferson's "wall of separation." The justices wrote, "No tax in any amount, large or small, can be levied to support any religious activities or institutions, whatever they may be called, or whatever form they may adopt to teach or practice religion."

THE COURTS AND SCHOOLS

Prayer in school was at the center of several high-profile court cases following the *Everson v. Board of*

Children ride a Catholic-school bus in the 1960s. U.S. courts have ruled that taxpayer money cannot be used for transportation costs associated with children attending church-run schools.

Education ruling. The Court handed down several rulings intended to define boundaries for religion in schools. Most of these cases were brought by people who were upset by school policies that seemed to place an emphasis on religion while excluding children who did not belong to that particular faith. Among these cases was *McCollum v. Board of Education of Champaign, Illinois.*

THE RIGHT TO DECLINE

In 1940, a community group called the Champaign Council on Religious Education was formed. The organization was made up of members of area Protestant, Catholic, and Jewish groups who wanted to bring classes on their faiths to local public schools. The Champaign Board of Education agreed to let them lead voluntary sessions once a week during school hours for students in the fourth through ninth grades. The classes took place inside the school, and parents had to give permission before their children could participate.

When Vashti McCollum's son reached the fourth grade, she decided she didn't want him to take part in the sessions. McCollum was an atheist and did not believe that her son should have to participate. As

THE SCOPES MONKEY TRIAL

In 1925, high school biology teacher John Scopes was arrested for teaching the theory of evolution. A newly passed Tennessee law forbade teaching any theory that contradicted creationism as described in the Bible. Supported by the American Civil Liberties Union (ACLU), Scopes challenged the constitutionality of the law.

The case represented a clash of traditional values based on religion versus the transforming forces of modernism and science. The dramatic, highly publicized trial pitted two of the nation's greatest orators against each other in court. Firebrand attorney Clarence Darrow represented the defense. Statesman William Jennings Bryan, a former candidate for U.S. president, argued for the prosecution.

Scopes was found guilty and ordered to pay a $100 fine, but in the eyes of many Americans, Darrow won the ideological battle. The case raised public debate and awareness of evolution. Though the Tennessee law remained in place until 1967, many states rejected pending antievolution legislation after the verdict.

the classes went on, she learned that her son was being singled out for not taking part. She requested that the school board end the classes, but the board refused. She filed a lawsuit against the board in 1945 on the grounds that the classes violated the First Amendment's establishment clause and the Fourteenth Amendment's equal protection clause.

McCollum's complaint to the local district court held that some of the Protestant denominations leading the classes had more power than others. By choosing who could lead the classes, they were showing favoritism toward a religion at the expense of others. The complaint also stated that the classes were not really voluntary because the schools pressured students to take them.

The Circuit Court of Champaign County disagreed with McCollum's complaint and ruled in January 1946 that the school district was not violating the Constitution. The Illinois Supreme Court also ruled against McCollum. The family did not give up, however, and appealed to the U.S. Supreme Court, which agreed to hear the case in 1947.

McCollum v. Board of Education of Champaign, Illinois was the first major ruling regarding the separation of church and state since the *Everson* case. Several religious groups, including the American Unitarian

Vashti McCollum, seen here sitting outside the Supreme Court building in 1947, protested voluntary religious education classes held at her son's public school in Champaign, Ill.

Association and the Baptist Joint Committee of Religious Liberty, filed briefs in support of the family's position.

THE RULING IN *MCCOLLUM*

The Court ultimately ruled 8–1 in McCollum's favor, handing down a ruling in March 1948 that the classes were unconstitutional. In the majority opinion, Justice Hugo Black wrote that the facts showed that tax-supported property was used for religious purposes and that the public school board worked closely with religious leaders to promote religious education. While the students were released from school for the duration of the classes, their release was conditional upon receiving religious education.

"This is beyond all question a utilization of the tax-established and tax-supported public school system to aid religious groups to spread their faith," Black wrote. "And it falls squarely under the ban of the First Amendment (made applicable to the States by the Fourteenth) as we interpreted it in *Everson v. Board of Education*."

The dissenting judge, Justice Stanley Forman Reed, opined that a narrow reading of the First

Amendment would have allowed the classes to continue. Reed particularly objected to the use of the "wall of separation" phrase in the decision. "A rule of law should not be drawn from a figure of speech," he wrote in his dissent.

Justice Stanley Reed, pictured here, cast the sole dissenting vote in the *McCollum* case.

The case changed the life that McCollum and her family led in Champaign. She lost her job as a dance instructor, and many of her neighbors stopped speaking to her. Trick-or-treaters pelted the McCollum house with vegetables, and someone killed the family's cat. McCollum later wrote a book about the case, titled *One Woman's Fight*, and served two terms as the president of the American Humanist Association.

CHAPTER FOUR

YEARS OF UPHEAVAL

T he *Everson v. Board of Education* decision resonated throughout the coming decades. When the decision was handed down, it was common for public school districts to have students begin the day with a non-denominational prayer. Instead of putting the question of whether religion belonged in taxpayer-funded schools to rest, the ruling stirred up strong feelings on both sides of the issue. Supporters of school prayer said

Dr. Martin Luther King Jr. leads a civil rights demonstration in 1960. The civil rights movement was energized by church congregations and their leaders.

that the government was intruding on their religious freedom. Opponents made the same argument, stating that they felt their rights were being violated because allowing prayer placed the faith of others above their own beliefs.

DEVOTION ON SCHOOL TIME

The next major ruling to tackle religion in public schools was the Supreme Court's decision in the case of *Zorach v. Clauson* in 1952. After the end of the *McCollum v. Board of Education* hearing, a New York City program was established that let public school students be released from class so that they could receive religious instruction or participate in devotional activities away from school grounds. The voluntary program released the children for forty-five minutes to an hour. The release was carried out with permission from parents, and the participating religious institutions shared attendance records with the schools. The students who did not take part were given activities to do while their classmates were away.

Parents who disagreed with the policy sued, arguing that the school district was violating the First and Fourteenth amendments by religious establishment. After the New York Supreme Court sided with the school district in its ruling, the parents appealed to the U.S. Supreme Court. This time, they argued that the state was supporting a religious education program and there was subtle pressure placed on students to take part. The city countered that all religious education took place away from school and the program was voluntary and no public funds went into it. Because of these factors, no establishment of religion took place.

The Court sided 6–3 with the school district in saying that the policy was constitutional. The majority opinion, written by Justice William O. Douglas, stated that unlike in *McCollum v. Board of Education*, the schools themselves were not being used for religious classes. They also found no evidence that students were pressured to participate.

William Douglas wrote the majority opinion in *Zorach v. Clauson*. His thirty-six years on the Supreme Court bench were marked by rulings that reflected his passion for individual rights.

Douglas stated in his opinion that while the separation of church and state should be absolute, the concept guaranteed only that the state should not be allowed to either interfere with the free exercise of religious faith or establish a religion. The New York policy did neither of those things. Instead, it merely accommodated the spiritual needs of students. If carried to an extreme, Douglas wrote, the separation of church and state could mean that firefighters and police officers would no longer be able to protect places of worship and prayers would not be allowed in public buildings.

The three dissenting justices—Hugo Black, Felix Frankfurter, and Robert Jackson—each stated that the school district failed to show that its policy was significantly different from the one presented in *McCollum*. In his dissent, Black stated that the arrangement was "not separation but combination of Church and State."

SCHOOL PRAYER

The first Supreme Court decision to address the question of prayer in schools was *Engel v. Vitale*. The case was filed in 1961 by the families of public school students in Hyde Park, New York, including the named plaintiff, Steven Engel. The families objected to a prayer written by the New York State Board of Regents that read, in part, "Almighty God, we acknowledge our dependence on Thee, and we beg Thou blessings upon us, our parents, our teachers, and our country." The prayer was read every day in the school in the presence of a teacher.

New York was not the only state to have prayers in school. At the time, schools in many states opened the day with a nondenominational prayer. Even today, many government ceremonies begin with such a prayer.

The plaintiffs in the Hyde Park case felt that the prayer was an attempt by the Board of Regents to introduce religion into public schools. Their argument was that it was in opposition to their religious practices and the children were being made to take part in a prayer that violated their religious beliefs. Backed by the ACLU, the families sued on the grounds that the prayer violated the establishment clause.

The district court and New York Supreme Court sided with the school district. The prayers could continue so long as they were voluntary and students weren't made to participate against the wishes of parents. The parents continued to appeal all the way to the U.S. Supreme Court.

Elementary school students in Newville, Pennsylvania, stand and bow their heads to pray during a moment of silence as part of their school day.

The case immediately took on a great deal of significance for both sides of the school prayer argument. The governments of twenty-two states filed letters in support of the New York Board of Regents, showing they backed prayer in schools. On the side of the parents, several groups, including the American Jewish Committee and Synagogue Council of America, wrote to ask the Court to overturn the earlier rulings and decide that the prayers were unconstitutional.

The justices of the Supreme Court sided with Engel and the other parents by a 6–1 vote. (Justice Frankfurter was incapacitated by a stroke that forced him to retire before the ruling could be handed down, and Justice Byron White stood aside during the hearing.) The justices found that the Regents prayer violated the establishment clause because it was written by government officials as part of a government program to further religious beliefs. Therefore, using the prayer on school grounds was a breach of the First Amendment. Justice Potter Stewart was the lone dissenting vote. He wrote in his opinion that he felt that allowing a voluntary prayer did not violate the Constitution and the Court was misreading the establishment clause.

With the ruling, the Supreme Court effectively ended state-sponsored prayer in public schools. However, the issue didn't go away. Many other cases would take up the constitutionality of prayer in public schools, as later courts worked to refine the broad ruling handed down in *Engel v. Vitale*.

BIBLICAL CONTROVERSY

In 1963, the Supreme Court issued another ruling that further defined the boundaries of prayer in school. *School District of Abington Township v. Schempp* shared similarities with *Engel v. Vitale*. The case was about a Pennsylvania law passed in 1949 that required public school students to read at least ten passages from the Bible while school was in session. Pennsylvania was one of five states that

PUBLIC REACTION

Public response to the *Engel v. Vitale* ruling was strong on both sides. The outcome became the subject of many newspaper columns and political cartoons. A number of groups, particularly those with Jewish and Baptist affiliations, were pleased with the ruling. Others spoke out against it. In a speech given in Utah soon after the ruling, Harvard Law School dean Erwin Griswold said the nation was Christian in its origins and the notion of religious tolerance was formed from Christian values. "But does the fact that we have officially adopted toleration as our standard mean that we must give up our history and our tradition?" Griswold asked.

The Harvard dean's views were shared by many Americans. A month after the ruling, the U.S. Senate spent two days holding hearings on *Engel v. Vitale*. By the end of the hearings, three constitutional amendments designed to permit school prayer were proposed. In the years that followed the *Engel v. Vitale* ruling, dozens of similar amendments were proposed that would have made publicly sponsored prayer a protected right. None ever gained enough support to pass.

required daily Bible reading, while twenty-five other states had laws allowing optional Bible reading. In eleven of those states, the laws had been declared unconstitutional.

In Abington Township, the school district required students to recite the Lord's Prayer after the Bible verse readings were finished. As with the Bible readings, students could be excused from taking part in the recitation of the prayer if they had a written note from their parents. Students themselves could not ask to be excused from the exercise. Anyone who attempted to protest the readings was disciplined, and teachers who refused to allow the readings could be fired.

A Unitarian named Edward Schempp sued the district over the law in 1958. Schempp's children had been among the students who were punished for refusing to participate in the readings. The Schempps had decided not to have their son and daughter excused from the readings because they feared that doing so would harm the relationship the kids had with other students.

The Schempp family won the case, but the school district appealed to the U.S. Supreme

Court, which called for a new hearing. After the first district court decision, Pennsylvania legislators passed a bill making the Bible readings optional. Parents could request in writing that their children not participate.

Ellery Schempp poses with a newspaper article concerning his part in an earlier debate over religion in public schools, in 2007.

Schempp was not appeased by the change and continued the suit. The school district again lost in district court and once again appealed. The case finally made it to the U.S. Supreme Court in 1962.

The Schempp family challenged the law on the grounds that it violated the establishment clause. By requiring the Bible readings, the state government was acting to establish a state religion, they said. The Supreme Court agreed with the Schempps. In an 8–1 ruling, the justices agreed that the school district showed definite favoritism toward Christianity and did not meet the state's required standard of neutrality. Instead, the schools were broadcasting a specific religious message. The Pennsylvania law was struck down.

At the same time as the *Schempp* case, the Court heard a similar case, *Murray* v. *Curlett*, which was brought by Madalyn Murray and her son William. The Murrays were atheists who challenged a 1905 Baltimore school board policy that called for the school day to start with a reading from the Bible or the Lord's Prayer.

Like the Schempps, they only brought the suit after protesting to officials. As in the *Schempp* case, the Murrays argued that the establishment clause was being violated. The school district's policy was basically requiring children to undergo religious education while attending public school. The Murrays lost the case but appealed, and the Supreme Court agreed to consolidate the case along with the *Schempp* case.

IMPACT OF THE *SCHEMPP* CASE

Abington Township v. Schempp served as an important milestone in the debate over the separation of church and state. The outcome of the case was very similar to that of *Engel v. Vitale*, including the reason for finding the Bible reading and prayer unconstitutional. However, in the *Schempp* ruling the Supreme Court took the important step of establishing a test for whether actions taken by local or state governments were constitutional.

In writing the majority opinion, Justice Tom Clark wrote that the Constitution required that all levels of government must remain neutral in matters concerning religion. In fact, all religions must be protected equally, with no preference shown to any faith. Clark established guidelines that could be used to determine whether a law was constitutional according to the establishment clause. In order for a statute to be constitutional, it would have to have a valid nonreligious purpose and should not advance or hinder a particular faith. Bible study and religion could have a place in schools if they were presented in an unbiased way as part of a secular education program. Religious practices held in public school would not be acceptable under the test set forth by the justices.

"While the Free Exercise Clause clearly prohibits the use of State Action to deny the rights of free exercise to anyone, it has never meant that a majority could use the machinery of the State to practice its beliefs," Clark wrote. In other words, the Constitution forbade any law on any level that was designed to use state institutions such as schools to make people follow a particular religious practice. Voluntary prayer and learning about religion were not mentioned in the opinion.

Justice William Brennan added a lengthy concurring opinion that became significant in later rulings. In his seventy-three-page opinion, Brennan focused on the history of the establishment clause and the intended purpose of the First and Fourteenth amendments. He felt that a proper understanding of the history of the clause was necessary in order to silence critics who held that prayer in schools and in other parts of public life was a tradition dating back to the ratification of the Bill of Rights. He cited the states that had passed similar laws to those in Pennsylvania, only to revoke them later. Brennan also noted the many diverse faiths practiced in the United States and cited them as a reason for not elevating one religion over others.

The lone dissenting opinion came from Justice Potter Stewart, who also had dissented in *Engel v. Vitale*. As in the earlier case, Stewart objected to the idea that the establishment clause was designated as more important than the free exercise clause. He also was unconvinced that Maryland and Pennsylvania had forced students to pray or read the Bible.

CHAPTER FIVE

RENEWED BATTLES

The *Schempp* ruling was the last major court decision of the 1960s to touch on the separation of church and state. Despite the strict guidelines set by the U.S. Supreme Court in its verdict regarding prayer in schools and state-sponsored religious activity, another wave of cases came about in the 1970s.

A TIME OF CHANGE

The Court's rulings in the *Engel*, *Schempp*, and *Murray* cases served as a rallying cry for many people who believed that religion should play a role in government. The number of people regularly attending religious services continued to go up. Politically motivated religious organizations also grew in number and stature.

Changes to the nation's religious fabric had become more evident during the 1960s. Mainstream Protestant, Catholic, and Jewish groups were often confronted by the fact that growing numbers of

Citizens protest the use of the phrase "under God" in the Pledge of Allegiance outside the Supreme Court building in 2004.

Americans practiced faiths such as Islam, Buddhism, and Hinduism, among others. They were no longer the majority that they had been just a few decades ago.

Some of the groups that emerged during this time were reacting to this broadening diversity. They wanted to make sure that their particular faiths did not lose influence in society. Some were motivated by the Supreme Court's rulings on school prayer and mobilized to bring their vision of the nation as one that was dominated by the beliefs of Christian and Jewish groups. Still others were galvanized by other social issues, including the debate over abortion. Many Roman Catholics and evangelical Christians disagreed with the 1973 Supreme Court ruling in *Roe v. Wade*, which struck down laws banning abortion, and became more politically active because of it.

PRIVATE SCHOOL, PUBLIC MONEY

The U.S. Supreme Court faced another debate over religion in public schools in 1971, when justices heard arguments in the case of *Lemon v. Kurtzman*. The case was centered upon a controversial 1968 Pennsylvania law called the Nonpublic Elementary and Secondary Education Act that gave the state's superintendent of public instruction the right to give

THE NATIONAL MOTTO

The United States did not have a national motto for more than 150 years. For much of the nation's history, the Latin phrase *E pluribus unum* ("From many, one") served as an unofficial motto. In 1956, President Dwight Eisenhower signed a bill into law designating the phrase "In God We Trust" as the nation's official motto. The phrase had been printed on money since the 1790s, and some already considered it the nation's motto.

The decision to make "In God We Trust" the nation's official motto was uncontroversial at the time, as many sought to set the United States apart from the Communist government of the Soviet Union. Since then, some have questioned whether the phrase violates the separation of church and state. In 1970, the Ninth District Court of Appeals ruled that it did not. The Supreme Court has never heard a case on the matter.

money to private schools to pay teacher salaries. Many of these private schools were operated by Catholic organizations, and the funds were supposed

Students line up at St. Augustine's Catholic school in Washington, D.C. Efforts to pay the salaries of private, religious school teachers have often been found unconstitutional by the Supreme Court.

to go to pay teachers for classroom time spent on secular subjects. The state could also cover the costs of any books or materials used in nonreligious classes.

The act required that for a teacher to be eligible for state reimbursement, he or she could only teach courses that were also offered in public schools and use only materials that could be found in those schools. Teachers also could not teach any classes that touched on religion.

A teacher named Alton Lemon filed suit against David Kurtzman, who was serving as Pennsylvania's acting superintendent of the Department of Public Instruction. Lemon saw the payments to religious schools as a violation of the establishment clause because they combined the interests of the state with those of a particular religious group. He believed the state was acting in the interest of a small section of its population, rather than for all of its people. A panel of three judges dismissed the suit, finding that the establishment and free exercise clauses were not violated. Lemon appealed.

The Supreme Court heard *Lemon v. Kurtzman* concurrently with two similar cases that originated in Rhode Island: *Earley v. DiCenso* and *Robinson v. DiCenso*. The two Rhode Island cases were brought over a 1969 law that let the state make salary payments to teachers in private schools, including those operated by churches. A state judicial panel had found that about 25 percent of Rhode Island students attended private schools. Nearly all of these children— about 95 percent—went to Roman Catholic schools. Among the private school teachers in the state, the bulk of the funds paid out went to fewer than three hundred educators. The state school board appealed the ruling, sending the case to the U.S. Supreme Court.

THE LEMON TEST

The Supreme Court ruled 8–0 (Justice Thurgood Marshall played no part in the ruling) that both statutes were unconstitutional. The justices decided that both laws resulted in entanglements between the state and religious institutions that were too deep to be constitutional. In their decision, they wrote, "In the absence of precisely stated constitutional prohibitions, we must draw lines with reference to the three main evils against which the Establishment Clause was intended to afford protection: 'sponsorship, financial support, and active involvement of the sovereign in religious activity.'"

As they came to a decision in the case, the justices established a test that could be used in future cases to decide whether a law violated the establishment clause. This standard, which came to be called the Lemon Test, consisted of three main questions: 1) Does the law have a secular legislative purpose?; 2) Does its primary effect advance or inhibit a particular religion?; and 3) Does the statute create an excessive government entanglement with religion? The justices found that the two Rhode Island cases and the Pennsylvania case all resulted in excessive entanglements of government and religion.

In the two Rhode Island cases, the entanglement was caused by the religious purpose of the church-sponsored schools. Elementary schoolchildren were seen as being particularly impressionable, bringing about the possibility that they could be influenced

A woman protests the teaching of intelligent design, which is based on the idea that life is so complex that it can only occur through acts of God.

by religious activities held in schools. Teachers who worked under the authority of religious institutions might be compelled to introduce the church's agenda into the classroom, giving the state less control over how religion and secular subjects would be kept separate. The state would have to closely monitor schools in order to ensure that religion did not make its way into secular education classes. School records would also have to be closely watched so that the state could make sure that public money was used for secular purposes.

The Pennsylvania law created similar problems, requiring a program of surveillance to guarantee that teachers did not stray from secular discussions and to make sure that funds for secular and religious programs remained separate. The Pennsylvania statute had another complication, in that it provided continuous direct funding to church-sponsored schools. This funding method created a relationship between religious institutions and the state government that was far too close to be constitutional.

The justices also concluded that one of the intentions of the First Amendment was to eliminate political divisions between different religions. The programs established by Pennsylvania and Rhode Island only served to deepen religious divisions because of the relatively small number of religious institutions involved. The Court held that these divisions would become more intense if the programs were allowed to continue.

Since the ruling, the Lemon Test has been used in many court cases. It is still in use today and functions as the main guide as to whether a law is constitutional. Critics have at times attacked the test. Some believe it plays too large a role in restricting religious practice and the Supreme Court overreached when it established the test. Others have criticized the Lemon Test because it has been inconsistently applied in court cases. Depending on the justices seated on the Court at any given time, the test has been applied either strictly or with a great deal of leniency toward state and local laws.

CHAPTER SIX

AFTER THE LEMON TEST

The Lemon Test did not put questions of the separation of church and state to rest, but it did provide some guidance for courts to follow. Church and state issues that arose during the 1970s, 1980s, and 1990s were often framed by previous Court decisions, particularly by *Schempp v. Abington* and *Engel v. Vitale*.

Groups that wanted a close relationship between government and religion, particularly Christianity, gathered momentum during the 1980s. Organizations such as the Moral Majority, Christian Coalition, and Focus on the Family became more influential as their members lobbied the government to support their causes. Their goals included returning prayer and religious instruction to public schools, overturning the *Roe v. Wade* verdict, which legalized abortion,

Newt Gingrich addresses a crowd in 1996 with the support of the Christian Coalition. Faith-based organizations such as the coalition have increasingly made their presence felt in the political arena.

and halting what they believed to be the moral decay of American society.

In 1980, Ronald Reagan was elected president with strong support from evangelical Christian voters. Reagan had the backing of several socially conservative Christian groups. During his campaign, he promised that he would restore prayer in public schools and end abortion. Neither effort was successful. During his first term in office, he sought a constitutional amendment that would have made prayer in school mandatory, but he never got much support in Congress for the proposal.

Advocates for a strict separation of church and state became more vocal during this period. The American Civil Liberties Union and Americans United for Separation of Church and State both challenged laws that they believed sought to establish one set of religious beliefs to the detriment of others. At the same time, the nation was becoming more religiously diverse as more immigrants began coming to the United States from countries where Christianity was not the dominant religion. Faiths such as Islam, Buddhism, and Hinduism became more prominent. In 1992, for example, the military commissioned its first Muslim chaplains and the U.S. Senate held its first Muslim prayer reading, despite the fact that Muslims had been a part of the nation for centuries. In time, representatives from other religious traditions would read prayers in the Capitol.

Also during this time, a movement had been growing toward finding a more prominent place for public prayer in society. This

A Muslim U.S. Army chaplain leads other followers of Islam in prayer. Though Muslim chaplains have been part of the military since the 1990s, their numbers remain small.

movement was in disagreement with the firm separation of church and state that the Supreme Court had
drawn in previous cases. Presidents Ronald Reagan
and George H. W. Bush each appointed new Supreme
Court justices whom many believed would reverse
earlier rulings that barred prayer and religious instruction from classrooms.

PUBLIC RELIGIOUS DISPLAYS

Although Christianity remains the dominant religion
in the United States, Americans practice a wide variety
of faiths, share in multiple traditions, and celebrate
numerous religious holidays. While the Constitution
forbids governments from establishing one religion
above others, the symbols and language of Christianity
are deeply woven into American culture. Through the
First Amendment, Americans are free to practice
Christianity or any other faith without fear of persecution. They can put up religious displays or pray in
public. The Constitution only restricts displays and
prayers that are led by government bodies or taxing
agencies. If a government department puts up a religiously themed display catering to one faith while
neglecting others, it could be found to be in violation
of the establishment clause.

Over time, Christian holidays such as Easter and Christmas have developed a decidedly secular tone. References to Santa Claus or the Easter Bunny are commonplace in the media, in stores, and even in schools. In fact, the model for the jolly, gift-giving Santa Claus was the early Christian figure Saint Nicholas the Wonder-Maker, although very little of that story is now connected to the modern Santa.

Both holidays have many religious symbols associated with them, such as Nativity scenes and Easter crosses. For the most part, the secular symbols of these holidays—such as Santa Claus for Christmas and bunnies for Easter—are considered acceptable and tend not to be challenged in court. Those that can be interpreted as showing favoritism to a religion are often targeted by advocates for the separation of church and state.

FAITH ON DISPLAY

The legality of religious Christmas decorations on public property was the focus of the 1984 U.S. Supreme Court case *Lynch v. Donnelly*, in which the city of Pawtucket, Rhode Island, was sued over its annual Christmas display. The city's display, which was a longstanding tradition in Pawtucket, included a Santa Claus house, candy canes, a Christmas tree, and a banner that read "Seasons Greetings." A crèche, or manger scene depicting the birth of Jesus Christ, was also part of the display, as it had been for more than forty years.

The display's mix of secular and religious symbols had long gone unchallenged, though some members of the community objected to the inclusion of the crèche in a display that was funded at the expense of taxpayers. However, in 1980, the Rhode Island chapter of the ACLU brought suit against the city on behalf of four residents, including Daniel Donnelly. Their suit named Pawtucket mayor Dennis Lynch as the defendant. Hearing the case the following year, a U.S. District Court found the display to be unconstitutional and called for it to be taken down. The city appealed, and the case was taken up by the U.S. Supreme Court in 1983.

The city based its case on the fact that the crèche was part of a much larger display that included Santa Claus, Rudolph the Red-Nosed Reindeer, and cutout cartoon characters. The crèche itself was only one element and was not displayed in an attempt to convert anyone or to promote religion. Taken as a whole, the city argued, the decorations were intended to draw shoppers to the downtown shopping district.

THE *LYNCH* DECISION

The justices applied the Lemon Test to the case and ruled 5–4 in March 1984 that the use of the crèche in Pawtucket's holiday display was constitutional. Even though the crèche had religious significance to Christians, it did not violate the establishment clause. The justices ruled that, when seen in the context of the holiday season, the crèche did not appear to be an attempt to deliver a religious message or elevate one faith above others. Instead, it simply showed the origins of Christmas and had "legitimate secular purposes."

"Taken together, these cases abundantly demonstrate the Court's concern to protect the genuine objectives of the Establishment Clause," Justice Warren Burger wrote in his majority opinion. "It is far too late in the day to impose a crabbed reading of the [Establishment] Clause on the country. We hold that, notwithstanding the religious significance of the crèche, the city of Pawtucket has not violated the Establishment Clause of the First Amendment."

Joining Burger in ruling for the city were justices Byron White, Lewis Powell, William Rehnquist, and Sandra Day O'Connor. The four justices who ruled in favor of Donnelly were William Brennan, Thurgood

The owner of the mobile Nativity display pictured here set up in a truck parked near a county courthouse to avoid disobeying an Indiana law against religious displays on public property.

Marshall, Harry Blackmun, and John Paul Stevens. In his dissent from the decision, Brennan wrote that the display did not pass the Lemon Test and that a holiday display of secular symbols could have been assembled without using religious symbols.

Pawtucket ultimately won the right to display its holiday scene, but it had sold the crèche to a private committee after the 1981 U.S. District Court ruling in which the display was ruled unconstitutional. The committee erected the display downtown, but this time it was on private property and therefore a constitutionally protected expression of faith.

THE ENDORSEMENT TEST

One of the lasting legacies of *Lynch v. Donnelly* was a concurring opinion by Justice O'Connor, which included a reading of the establishment clause that came to be known as the Endorsement Test. O'Connor sought to clarify the Lemon Test standard that had been used and directly address public displays such as Pawtucket's crèche.

The Endorsement Test centers on the question of whether a public display shows approval or disapproval of a particular religion to the exclusion of others. Any government action that creates a perception that the government body is endorsing or showing disapproval of a religion would be unconstitutional. "Endorsement sends a message to non-adherents that they are outsiders, not full members of the political community, and an accompanying message to adherents that they are insiders, favored members of the political community," O'Connor wrote in her opinion.

Ultimately, the ruling was significant for the Court's refusal to take a hard line on the establishment clause. A display that included figures from one faith's traditions would be permitted, so long as the intention was secular and not religious and it did not represent any government entanglement.

76

PUTTING THE ENDORSEMENT TEST TO THE TEST

The Endorsement Test would be used in future Supreme Court cases, sometimes on its own and at other times as part of the Lemon Test. One of the first rulings in which it played a part was *County of Allegheny v. American Civil Liberties Union* (1989).

The ACLU had sued over two holiday displays located on public property in downtown Pittsburgh, Pennsylvania. One of the displays was a crèche that had been donated by a Roman Catholic group and placed on the staircase of the county courthouse. Above the manger was a banner reading "Gloria in excelsis Deo!" ("Glory to God in the highest!"). The other display was a large Hanukkah menorah that had been donated by a Jewish group and was located near the City-County Building.

The Supreme Court issued a complicated decision in the case, ruling 5–4 that the Nativity scene was unconstitutional because it failed both the Lemon Test and the Endorsement Test. It violated the establishment clause because its clear purpose was to endorse Christianity. Unlike the crèche in *Lynch v. Donnelly*, there were no other decorations alongside it to give it any kind of historical or cultural context.

Regarding the menorah display, the justices ruled 6–3 that it could remain where it was because of its physical placement outside the public buildings. The

THOU SHALT NOT POST COMMANDMENTS

Stone v. Graham was the first case that the Supreme Court heard on the use of the Ten Commandments in public schools. A Kentucky state law required that the commandments—taken from the Bible and including behavioral guidelines such as "Thou shalt not steal" and "Thou shalt not kill"—be posted in every public school classroom. Sydell Stone and other parents filed a suit against the state school supervisor to have them taken down. The Supreme Court ruled 5–4 in favor of the parents. In their ruling, the justices found that along with secular matters, such as theft and murder, the commandments also included rules about how to worship God. The ruling would have an impact on future cases relating to the display of the commandments in schools. Even though the documents were bought with private funds and donated by schools, the act of displaying them served as an endorsement of religion.

menorah was located near a Christmas tree and a sign that endorsed liberty. In such a setting, they decided, the menorah served as a secular symbol of the winter holiday season and did not overtly endorse the Jewish faith.

The case was hardly the last word on public religious displays. Similar cases continued to crop up for years to come. Court challenges to religiously themed decorations and displays featuring the Ten Commandments were often the catalysts for these cases.

CONTINUING SCHOOL CONFLICTS

The separation of church and state continues to be a major issue in schools. During the 1980s and 1990s, the Supreme Court handed down several rulings dealing with religious expression in schools and universities. As in previous years, prayer in school was the focal point in many of these cases.

In the case of *Wallace v. Jaffree*, a man named Ishmael Jaffree sued the school board of Mobile County, Alabama, over a state law that allowed teachers to use one minute of each school day for prayer or meditation. The law, which was passed by the state legislature in 1981, modified the language of

Ishmael Jaffree (*left*) seen here with his lawyer on the steps of the Supreme Courthouse in 1984, sought to overturn a law allowing a moment of silence in Alabama public schools.

an existing law that had allowed a moment of silence at the beginning of each day. Jaffree, an agnostic, argued that two of his three children were exposed to Christian religious teachings by several educators who led students in prayer on a daily basis. When they did not take part, they were ostracized by their classmates. Jaffree had repeatedly asked that the practice be stopped, but the school district denied his requests.

The Supreme Court ruled 6–3 that the Alabama law violated the endorsement clause. Justices applied the Lemon Test in the case and found that the Alabama law did not serve any secular purpose. In writing the majority opinion, Justice John Paul Stevens stated that the law ignored the state's constitutional duty to stay neutral in religious matters and it represented an endorsement of religion in public schools. The Court made a distinction between allowing children a moment of silence that they could use for voluntary prayer during the day and a time that was specifically set aside to pray or meditate. This showed definite favoritism to particular religious practices.

Stevens was joined in his opinion by justices William Brennan, Thurgood Marshall, Lewis Powell, Harry Blackmun, and Sandra Day O'Connor. Justices William Rehnquist, Warren Burger, and Byron White dissented from the majority opinion. In writing his dissent, Burger pointed out that the state law did not endorse religion because the prayer was voluntary.

THE ARRIVAL OF THE COERCION TEST

The case of *Lee v. Weisman* introduced another test for courts to use in deciding cases dealing with the separation of church and state. The case began in 1989, when school principal Robert Lee invited a Jewish rabbi to lead a prayer at the graduation ceremony for Nathan Bishop Middle School in Providence, Rhode Island. The parents of a student named Deborah Weisman sued to block the prayer from taking place, but the Rhode Island District Court denied their request. The rabbi spoke at the event, which the Weismans attended.

After the ceremony, the district court ruled in favor of the family and the school district appealed, sending the case to the First Circuit Court of Appeals. The court of appeals also ruled against the school district, stating that the use of prayer at official school functions violated all three parts of the Lemon Test. The school district then appealed to the U.S. Supreme Court, arguing that the prayer was voluntary because students did not have to stand for the prayer and participation in the graduation ceremony was not required.

Some watchers of the Court expected that the justices would find in favor of the school district. Justice Anthony Kennedy, who had been appointed in 1988, had criticized earlier rulings on the separation of church and state. Many believed that he would side with the more conservative justices on the Court and rule for the school district, which would limit the effectiveness of the precedents set by earlier decisions, such as *Engel v. Vitale*.

Ultimately, the Court ruled 5–4 in favor of the Weismans. Justice Kennedy wrote the majority opinion, in which he drew a distinction between the practice of using prayer to open legislative sessions and situations like the graduation ceremony. At legislative sessions, Kennedy decided, the people taking part in the prayer are all adults who are free to choose whether or not to participate. Graduation ceremonies, on the other hand, come with numerous pressures from parents and peers to participate.

The Court also ruled that children are highly susceptible to coercion through the schools, making it necessary to carefully examine situations involving the establishment clause and educational institutions. The decision was used to formulate what came to be called the Coercion Test. The test is now used to determine whether pressure is being used to make an individual participate in an activity with religious undertones.

"What to most believers may seem nothing more than a reasonable request that the nonbeliever respect their religious practices, in a school context may appear to the nonbeliever or dissenter to be an attempt to employ the machinery of the State to enforce a religious orthodoxy," Kennedy wrote.

The Coercion Test joined the Lemon Test and the Endorsement Test as the three main criteria that the Supreme Court now uses to decide separation of church and state issues. All three tests would be used in the coming years to decide cases involving religion in schools and religious displays on public property.

THE RELIGIOUS FREEDOM RESTORATION ACT

The push to give prayer and religious acts a greater role in society led to the passage of a law called the Religious Freedom Restoration Act. Passed by Congress in 1993 behind widespread support, the act reinstated the Sherbert Test, which was a 1960s interpretation of the First Amendment's free exercise clause that was used to prevent laws that place a burden on an individual's right to practice his or her religion. The act states that a religiously neutral law can have a negative impact on a person's ability to practice his or her faith. The act is applicable to all religions.

States are allowed to pass or enforce laws considered "burdensome" if they are used to advance some compelling goal and are the least restrictive means of accomplishing the objective. The act is used in a variety of ways and has been cited in a range of court cases, including those involving zoning laws that churches find restrictive and prison rules against wearing certain types of clothing.

CHAPTER SEVEN

OLD TENSIONS IN A NEW ERA

Challenges to Supreme Court rulings that favored the separation of church and state continued through the 1990s and into the twenty-first century. Efforts to overturn rulings such as *Engel v. Vitale* intensified after George W. Bush was elected president in 2000.

Bush was elected with strong support from religious conservatives, and he signed several laws that favored positions held by these groups. These included laws that banned

President George W. Bush signs the Unborn Victims of Violence Act into law. Opponents argued that the law could be used to restrict abortion rights.

late-term abortions and research using human stem cells, which some religious groups opposed because the cells were often taken from aborted fetuses.

Arguments about religion in schools and public religious displays have continued into the twenty-first century. The Supreme Court has ruled on a variety of cases on these topics in recent years. Justices have dealt with controversies surrounding prayer in schools, public funding for religious institutions, public displays, and religious teachings. In these cases, they have sought the guidance provided in earlier rulings.

A TAXING SITUATION

The question of whether it is constitutional to offer public financial support for churches and religious organizations has been addressed by the Supreme Court on several occasions. The case of *Arizona Christian School Tuition Organization v. Winn* began with the passage of a 1997 Arizona state law that brought the debate to the fore yet again. The law allowed people to receive tax credits if they made donations to school tuition groups that provided scholarships to students who attended private schools. Residents could contribute to many types of tuition funds, including some that placed students only in certain kinds of schools, such as those run by religious organizations.

In 2010, a group of taxpayers that included a woman named Kathleen Winn filed a lawsuit in federal district court in which they claimed that the tuition program violated the establishment clause because a large amount of the donated money went to students who attended religious schools. The district court ruled that the establishment clause was not violated because the law allowed residents to receive tax credits for donations to any tuition organization and did not favor those with ties to religious schools.

The U.S. Supreme Court heard the case in 2010 and issued its ruling the following spring. The justices ruled 5–4 that the taxpayers did not have legal standing to file suit in the case because they couldn't prove that the tax money was singled out for use by religious groups. Justices John Roberts, Clarence Thomas, Antonin Scalia, Anthony Kennedy, and Samuel Alito all ruled in favor of the Arizona law.

"This Court has rejected the general proposition that an individual who has paid taxes has a 'continuing, legally cognizable interest in ensuring that those funds are not used by the Government in a way that violates the Constitution,'" Justice Kennedy wrote in the majority opinion. Any damages or harm that the taxpayers claimed would be speculation because any benefits for the religious organizations came in the form of tax credits, not outright payments.

DISPLAYED WITH INTENT

Displays of the Ten Commandments are often challenged in court. As told in a biblical account, the commandments represent a set of rules of behavior passed down from God to the prophet Moses. The commandments are one of the touchstones of Christianity and Judaism—and they are sometimes said to be the basis of the American legal system. For this reason, religious groups sometimes work to have them displayed in public places, particularly in courthouses and schools.

In 2004, the American Civil Liberties Union sued three counties in Kentucky for displaying the commandments in their courthouses and in public schools. The ACLU argued that the displays violated the establishment clause because they represented an attempt to establish a religion. The counties responded by adopting official statements that stated the displays were meant to acknowledge the Ten Commandments as the basis of the state's laws.

The Ten Commandments are placed amid historic state documents in a Kentucky courthouse in 2001. Controversies over whether displays such as this promote religion have erupted for years.

A district court applied the Lemon Test in the case and found the displays to be in violation of the First Amendment, thereby forcing the counties to make changes to the exhibits. The commandments were then displayed alongside documents that are important to United States and state history, including the Bill of Rights, the Declaration of Independence, "The Star-Spangled Banner," and the Preamble to the Kentucky Constitution.

In appealing the ruling, the counties asked the Supreme Court to set aside the Lemon Test. The Court ruled 5–4 that the displays were unconstitutional, with the majority agreeing to keep the Lemon Test intact in the case because they felt it was important to examine a government's intentions when displaying documents. In his majority opinion, Justice David Souter wrote that the commandments were a sacred text and their placement in classrooms represented an establishment of religion. Even after linking the courthouse displays to other historical documents, the counties were still in

POSITION CAN BE EVERYTHING

At the same time that the Supreme Court issued its ruling in the Kentucky case, the justices also decided another Ten Commandments case, this one called *Van Orden v. Perry*. A Ten Commandments monument had been given to the state and displayed outside the Texas State Capitol. A man named Thomas Van Orden sued to have the monument removed. Ultimately, the Supreme Court ruled 5–4 to let it remain in place.

Why would this display be allowed to stay, while those in Kentucky had to be removed? The Texas monument was situated in a park that included thirty-eight other monuments and historical markers, giving it a broader context than the message of the commandments alone. Additionally, the Texas display featured prominent symbols used by the civic group that had donated it, thus making it clear that it wasn't provided by the state government.

violation of the First Amendment because they still carried a religious message.

SEPARATION IN THE FUTURE

The United States has become a much more religiously diverse nation since its founding. A 2012 Pew Research poll shows that more than 78 percent of U.S. adults identify as Christians, while close to 5 percent identify as belonging to another religion. Another 16 percent identified as "unaffiliated." Of those respondents who called themselves Christian, slightly more than 51 percent identified themselves as Protestant. Approximately 28 percent stated they have left the faith that they were born into.

The Supreme Court is charged with making sure that all of the nation's faiths are protected and their members can worship freely. The justices also have the difficult task of ensuring that the practices and beliefs of one religion are not placed above those of others, whether by accident or intent.

The Supreme Court, which had taken a firm line on the separation of church and state during the 1960s and 1970s, has shown some latitude in recent years. One case in which the justices showed flexibility was *Salazar v. Buono* (2010). The case centered on whether a memorial cross placed on federal land in the Mojave National Reserve violated the Constitution. The cross was erected in 1934 by the Veterans of Foreign Wars to commemorate those killed during World War I (1914–1918). Ultimately, the Court ruled 5–4 that the cross could stay on public land. "The goal of avoiding governmental endorsement [of religion] does not require eradication of all religious symbols in the

Pennsylvania protesters rally against the Affordable Care Act in 2012. The law's controversial birth control mandate has sparked debate, once again, over the separation of church and state.

public realm," Justice Anthony Kennedy wrote in the majority opinion.

Issues relating to prayer in school and the display of religious symbols are likely to come up before the courts again. The U.S. Supreme Court will also hear challenges by religious groups related to the Affordable Care Act, passed in 2010. Religious organizations and business owners have already filed suit to halt a part of the law stating that they must provide insurance coverage that includes birth control, which goes against some beliefs. The challenges to this law will open a new set of questions about the First Amendment, the freedom to practice religion, and the separation of church and state.

GLOSSARY

abolish To officially end or stop something, such as a law or practice.

amendment A change or addition to a document, such as a bill or constitution.

clause A distinct part of a formal document.

coercion The act of making something happen, or making someone do something, using force or threats.

convert To bring over from one belief, view, or party to another.

denomination A religious organization whose congregations are united by a set of beliefs and practices.

discriminate To unfairly treat a person or group of people differently from other people or groups.

doctrine A set of beliefs or ideas that are taught or believed to be true.

endorse To express support or approval of in an open and public manner.

establish To make a church a national or state religion.

infringe To wrongly restrict or limit something, such as a person's rights.

interpret To conceive in the light of individual belief, judgment, or circumstance.

legislature A body of officials that have been elected or chosen to make, change, or repeal laws.

persecute To treat someone unfairly or cruelly because of race or religious or political beliefs.

precedent Something done or said that can serve as an example or rule in similar cases in the future.

prohibit To forbid by authority.

ratify To confirm by expressing approval or consent.

solicit To ask strangers and members of the general public for something, especially money or assistance.

unconstitutional Illegal or not allowed under the constitution of a country or government.

FOR MORE INFORMATION

American Civil Liberties Union
125 Broad Street, 18th Floor
New York NY 10004
(212) 549-2500
Web site: http://www.aclu.org
The American Civil Liberties Union is a nonpartisan
   organization dedicated to preserving individual
   rights as guaranteed by the U.S. Constitution.

Bill of Rights Institute
200 North Glebe Road, Suite 200
Arlington, VA 22203
(703) 894-1776
Web site: http://www.billofrightsinstitute.org
The Bill of Rights Institute's mission is to educate
   people about the words and ideas of America's
   founders, the liberties guaranteed in founding
   documents, and the continued impact of these
   principles.

Canadian Museum for Human Rights
400-269 Main Street
Winnipeg, MB R3C 1B3
Canada
(877) 877-6037

Web site: http://humanrightsmuseum.ca

The Canadian Museum for Human Rights is envisioned as a place where people can engage in discussion and commit to taking action against hate and oppression.

James Madison's Montpelier
P.O. Box 911
Orange, VA 22960
(540) 672-2728
Web site: http://www.montpelier.org

Once home to James Madison and his wife, Dolly, Montpelier today houses a center for learning about Madison and his vision for a constitutional government.

Library of Congress
101 Independence Avenue SE
Washington, DC 20540
(202) 707-5000
Web site: http://www.loc.gov

The Library of Congress's collections contain many of the United States' most important documents.

National Constitution Center
Independence Mall

525 Arch Street
Philadelphia, PA 19106
(205) 409-6600
Web site: http://constitutioncenter.org
The National Constitution Center is dedicated to pro-
    moting a better understanding of and appreciation
    for the Constitution, its history, and its contemporary
    relevance.

Parliament of Canada
Information Service
Ottawa, ON K1A 0A9
Canada
(613) 992-4793
Web site: http://www.parl.gc.ca
The Canadian Parliament was established in 1867 and
    serves as the nation's legislative body. It is modeled
    after the British Parliament.

Smithsonian National Museum of American History
1000 Jefferson Drive SW
Washington, DC 20004
(202) 633-1000
Web site: http://americanhistory.si.edu
The National Museum of American History collects
    artifacts to preserve for the American people a
    record of their past.

U.S. National Archives and Records Administration
8601 Adelphi Road
College Park, MD 20740
(866) 272-6272
Web site: http://www.archives.gov
The National Archives and Records Administration
    preserves government documents and records that
    have historical or legal significance.

WEBSITES

Due to the changing nature of Internet links, Rosen
Publishing has developed an online list of websites
related to the subject of this book. This site is updated
regularly. Please use this link to access the list:

http://www.rosenlinks.com/UUSC/Chur

FOR FURTHER READING

Barnes, Trevor. *World Faiths: Christianity*. New York, NY: Kingfisher, 2013.

Burgan, Michael. *Cornerstones of Freedom: The U.S. Constitution*. Danbury, CT: Children's Press, 2011.

Conway, John. *A Look at the First Amendment: Freedom of Speech and Religion*. Berkeley Heights, NJ: Enslow Publishers, 2008.

CQ Press, ed. *Student's Guide to the U.S. Supreme Court*. Washington, DC: CQ Press, 2010.

DiPrimio, Pete. *The Judicial Branch*. Hockessen, DE: Mitchell Lane Publishers, 2011.

Fradin, Dennis. *The Bill of Rights*. Salt Lake City, UT: Benchmark Books, 2008.

Harrison, Geoffrey, and Thomas F. Scott. *Church and State* (Great Debates). Chicago, IL: Norwood House Press, 2013.

Jacobs, Thomas A. *What Are My Rights? Q&A About Teens and the Law*. Minneapolis, MN: Free Spirit Publishing, 2011.

Jones, Molly. *The First Amendment: Freedom of Speech, the Press, and Religion*. New York, NY: Rosen Publishing, 2011.

Langley, Myrtle. *DK Eyewitness Books: Religion*. New York, NY: DK Publishing, 2012.

Lawrence, Jerome, and Robert E. Lee. *Inherit the Wind*. New York, NY: Ballantine Books, 2007.

Leavitt, Aime. *The Bill of Rights*. Hockessen, DE: Mitchell Lane Publishers, 2011.

Madani, Hamed. *The Supreme Court and the Judicial Branch: How the Federal Courts Interpret Our Laws*. Berkeley Heights, NJ: Enslow Publishers, 2013.

Nelson, Drew. *Meet the Supreme Court*. New York, NY: Gareth Stevens Publishing, 2012.

Raatma, Lucia. *The Bill of Rights*. New York, NY: Children's Press, 2011.

Ransom, Candice. *Who Wrote the U.S. Constitution?: And Other Questions About the Constitutional Convention of 1787*. Minneapolis, MN: Lerner Publishing Group, 2010.

Sirimarco, Elizabeth. *Thomas Jefferson: Our Third President*. Mankato, MN: Child's World, 2009.

Somervill, Barbara. *The Life and Times of James Madison* (Profiles in American History). Hockessen, DE: Mitchell Lane Publishers, 2008.

Swain, Gwenyth. *Documents of Freedom: A Look at the Declaration of Independence, the Bill of Rights, and the U.S. Constitution*. Minneapolis, MN: Lerner Publishing Group, 2012.

Wilson, Shaun Michael, and Benjamin Dickson. *Fight the Power: A Visual History of Protest Among the English Speaking Peoples*. New York, NY: Seven Stories Press, 2013.

BIBLIOGRAPHY

Beckman, Joanne. "Religion in Post–World War II America." National Humanities Center, October 2000. Retrieved November 6, 2013 (http://nationalhumanitiescenter.org/tserve/twenty/tkeyinfo/trelww2.htm).

Carmel, Jeffrey J. "Pawtucket's Crèche Shifts to Private Park." *Christian Science Monitor*, October 20, 1983. Retrieved November 6, 2013 (http://www.csmonitor.com/1983/1020/102033.html).

Curwen, Thomas. "A Mojave Desert Cross Brings a Lot of Things to Bear." *Los Angeles Times*, October 21, 2012. Retrieved November 6, 2013 (http://articles.latimes.com/2012/oct/21/local/la-me-mojave-cross-20121022).

Davis, Kenneth C. "America's True History of Religious Tolerance." *Smithsonian*, October 2010. Retrieved November 6, 2013 (http://www.smithsonianmag.com/history-archaeology/Americas-True-History-of-Religious-Tolerance.html).

de Lama, George. "Reagan Sees an 'Uphill Battle' for Prayer in Public Schools." *Chicago Tribune*, June 7, 1985. Retrieved November 6, 2013 (http://articles.chicagotribune.com/1985-06-07/

news/8502050842_1_supreme-court-vietnam
-nicaragua).

The Economist. "Endorsing the Endorsement Test."
October 8, 2013. Retrieved November 6, 2013
(http://www.economist.com/blogs/democracyin
america/2013/10/religious-liberty-and-supreme
-court).

Evans, M. Stanton. *The Theme Is Freedom:
Religion, Politics, and the American Tradition.*
Washington, DC: Regnery Publishing, 1994.

Feldman, Stephen M. *Please Don't Wish Me a
Merry Christmas: A Critical History of the
Separation of Church and State.* New York, NY:
New York University Press, 1997.

Frankel, Marvin E. *Faith and Freedom: Religious
Liberty in America.* New York, NY: Hill and
Wang, 1994.

Gaddy, C. Welton, and Barry W. Lynn. *First
Freedom First: A Citizens' Guide to Protecting
Religious Liberty and the Separation of Church
and State.* Boston, MA: Beacon Press, 2008.

Haynes, Charles. "50 Years Later, How School-Prayer
Ruling Changed America." First Amendment Center,
June 29, 2012. Retrieved November 6, 2013 (http://
www.firstamendmentcenter.org/50-years-later-how
-school-prayer-ruling-changed-america).

Hutson, James. "A Wall of Separation." *Library of Congress Information Bulletin*, June 1998. Retrieved November 6, 2013 (http://www.loc .gov/loc/lcib/9806/danbury.html).

Lacorne, Denis. *Religion in America: A Political History*. New York, NY: Columbia University Press, 2011.

Levy, Leonard W. *The Establishment Clause: Religion and the First Amendment*. 2nd ed. Chapel Hill, NC: University of North Carolina Press, 1994.

Lupu, Ira C., et. al. "Religious Displays and the Courts." Pew Research Center, June 2007. Retrieved November 6, 2013 (http://www .pewforum.org/files/2007/06/religious -displays.pdf).

Masci, David. "In Brief: *Arizona Christian School Tuition Organization v. Winn* and *Arizona Department of Revenue v. Winn*." Pew Research Center, October 19, 2010. Retrieved November 6,2013 (http://www.pewforum.org/2010/10/19/in- brief-arizona-christian-school-tuition -organization-v-winn-and-arizona-department -of-revenue-v-winn).

Moughty, Sarah. "'In God We Trust' Reaffirmed as National Motto... Again." *Frontline*, November

4, 2011. Retrieved November 6, 2013 (http://
pbs.org/wgbh/pages/frontline/religion/god-in
-america/in-god-we-trust-reaffirmed-as
-national-motto-again).

Pew Research Center. "U.S. Religious Landscape
Survey." February 2008. Retrieved November 6,
2013 (http://religions.pewforum.org/pdf/report
-religious-landscape-study-full.pdf).

Wright, Jonathan A. *Separation of Church and
State*. Santa Barbara, CA: Greenwood, 2010.

INDEX

ABOUT THE AUTHOR

Jason Porterfield is a journalist and writer living in Chicago, Illinois. He graduated from Oberlin College, where he majored in English, history, and religion. He has written more than twenty books for Rosen Publishing, including several covering historical subjects such as the Lincoln-Douglas debates and the Treaty of Guadalupe-Hidalgo.

PHOTO CREDITS